I0438394

National Security Policy Proceedings

Volume 4

Winter 2010

FRANK J. GAFFNEY, JR.
Publisher

BEN LERNER
Editor-in-Chief

ADAM SAVIT
Associate Editor

securefreedom.org

CONTENTS

Note from the Editor

For the past several years, the Center for Security Policy has been privileged to host its biweekly National Security Group Lunch on Capitol Hill. The purpose of the lunch is to bring together national security practitioners from Congress, the executive branch, the think-tank community, grassroots organizations, the private sector, and elsewhere, to receive expert briefings and discuss strategies for advancing the national security model that Ronald Reagan referred to as "Peace through Strength."

Over the years, the lunches have been addressed by Members of Congress and key members of their staff, former Assistant Secretaries of Defense and State, White House advisors, bestselling national security authors, and preeminent scholars in topics such as the ideology of jihad, North Korea, Russia, nuclear deterrence, Afghanistan, border security, Latin America, the Patriot Act, and the International Criminal Court, among many others.

National Security Policy Proceedings represents the Center's compilation of transcripts of remarks given by featured speakers at these gatherings. In some cases, speakers have chosen to submit their remarks to Proceedings as original articles. Additionally, Proceedings includes book reviews of recently published national security-themed books, reviewed by eminent scholars in the field. In publishing Proceedings, the Center has sought to provide the reader with authoritative yet accessible commentary on the most pressing issues of national security, foreign affairs, defense policy, and homeland security. Because the speakers and those in attendance are routinely in contact with one another and are often collaborating on analytical and educational efforts, it is our intention that Proceedings give the reader a unique window into how those in the national security policy community convey and exchange ideas with one another, among friends and colleagues.

We are pleased to present this winter 2010 issue of Proceedings, and we look forward to continuing to utilize this publication to make a significant contribution to the national security discourse.

Ben Lerner
Editor-in-Chief

A Biopreparedness Primer

TEVI TROY

President Barack Obama announced in his 2010 State of the Union address "a new initiative that will give us the capacity to respond faster and more effectively to bioterrorism or an infectious disease — a plan that will counter threats at home and strengthen public health abroad."

This past August, Health and Human Services Secretary Kathleen Sebelius issued a report following up on the State of the Union promise. As biopreparedness was a key issue for the Bush administration as well, it is worth looking at the background of this relatively rare instance of the 44th president continuing to pursue the policies of his predecessor.

Tevi Troy is a Visiting Senior Fellow at the Hudson Institute and former Deputy Secretary of Health and Human Services. This article was based on remarks he gave at the CSP National Security Group Lunch on 30 July, 2010.

Biopreparedness is often considered to be the "unwanted step-child" of the security industry. While the Defense Department and the Department of Homeland Security are, of course, focused on the issue, they share responsibility for it with the Department of Health and Human Services, especially the relatively new Biomedical Advanced Research and Development Authority (BARDA), created by Congress in 2006.

BIOTERROR HISTORY

While BARDA may be new, the phenomenon of bioterrorism dates back to 600 B.C., when Assyrian warriors started the practice of poisoning their enemy's water supplies with rye ergot, a toxic fungus. Bioterrorism was seen again nearly 2,000 years later when the Tartars launched bodies infected with the Plague over the walls of the city during their siege of Caffa.

Bioweaponry saw action on American soil in 1763, when British Colonel Henry Bouquet used smallpox against the Native Americans during the French and Indian War. Two centuries later, bioweapons research played an integral part in the defense strategy against the Soviets.

The United States ended its bioweapon research programs after the Vietnam War. This began a long quiet period during which the U.S. did not think too much about bioterrorism, either offensively or defensively. Recently, however, the September 11th attacks and the anthrax scares of 2001 have brought bioterrorism back onto the radar screen.

THE NATURE OF BIOLOGICAL WARFARE

There are many important differences between biological and conventional warfare. First and foremost, it's asymmetrical. As we saw with the anthrax scares of 2001, with bio-weaponry, a small, non-state actor with limited financial resources can cause enormous damage to a much larger target. The anthrax attacks of 2001 cost as little as $2,500 to produce, and, while certainly beyond my area of expertise, were not terribly complicated to create chemically. These attacks, while simple, shut down Capitol Hill, nearly immobilized the postal service, and caused a number of deaths. Second, the window of time for an effective response is much smaller. To further complicate things, the first responders – who may not be soldiers, but are instead doctors or

We must have the civil defense and distribution infrastructure necessary to effectively produce and distribute the appropriate counter and preventive measures. No matter how ingenious or effective a medication is, one dose of the medication that's stored in El Paso, Texas does no good for a thousand people infected in New York City.

EMT's – are put at risk.

Finally, panic plays a large role as well. While war-gaming in the Bush administration about potential CBRN (chemical, biological, radiological, or nuclear) threat scenarios, one of the surprising side effects we found was a large contingent of the "worried-well." These were people who had not been harmed by the attack, but nevertheless swamped hospitals because they were worried they had been affected. In our exercises, these "worried-well" patients clogged hospitals and sickrooms, and significantly delayed response times. As a result, the U.S. has subsequently included initiatives to ensure we are prepared for these patients, and know how to respond most effectively.

The potential attacks are not limited to the U.S. alone, and anthrax is not the only potential weapon. Ricin was found in the Paris subway system just a few years ago. The "Dirty Bomber" made headlines in 2003. Anthrax-spiked heroin has been recently found across Europe and England. As a thought experiment, consider this: What if the 2010 car-bomb attempt in Times Square had involved a dirty bomb? It would have resulted in the infection of thousands of New Yorkers, many without their knowledge.

THE U.S. RESPONSE

Fortunately, the U.S. government has dramatically increased its bioterrorism awareness from its post-Vietnam state. In 2001, the government increased funding for bioterror research to over $500 million. One year later, the Bioterrorism Act of 2002 assigned various responsibilities to different agencies and parts of the government in an effort to unify and streamline our defense against bioterrorism. 2004's Project Bioshield made it easier to develop and stockpile biological countermeasures.

These legislative efforts have helped us develop an effective bio-defense strategy, which must have three key components. The first is vigilance. There must be a commitment by the government to make sure biodefense is maintained. It will take time and manpower, but it's money well spent. We must also stay ahead of the curve techono-logically. There are many different potential bioweapons available cur-rently, and even more that can be potentially manufactured. Feasibil-ity studies can help determine what the most likely choices are, but in the end there are many options. A terrorist agent can pick any number of different potential bioweapons; we must be able to defend against all of them. Finally, we must have the civil defense and distribution infrastructure necessary to effectively produce and distribute the ap-propriate counter and preventive measures. No matter how ingenious or effective a medication is, one dose of the medication that's stored in El Paso, Texas does no good for a thousand people infected in New York City.

It's important to note that this is not just an American problem. With increasing globalization, it's possible for non-targeted nations to be affected by a bioterror attack. Consider the recent SARS outbreak in China. SARS cost the Asian nations affected a minimum of $11 billion. On average, there was an economic loss of over $2 million per person with SARS. While this was a naturally occurring outbreak, the spread-mechanics and the effects of globalization would be nearly identical to those of a planned attack. For comparison, the Brookings Institute has estimated that during an H1N1 pandemic in America, there would be a loss of between $10 billion and $47 billion in US economic activity.

With this in mind, it is worth looking at the recent swine flu outbreak and the government's response to it. The death toll was kept to fewer than 20,000 individuals worldwide, which was far lower than previously predicted. It's also a relatively small number when you consider previous outbreaks. The Hong Kong Flu of 1968 killed over 1 million people, and the Asian Flu of 1958 had nearly 2 million casualties. The low death toll can be attributed in part to the preparedness of the U.S. government. Starting in 2005, President Bush had a $7 billion strategy which included investments in vaccines, antivirals, domestic preparedness, and international cooperation.

While planning these investments and developing our strategy, the U.S. used what's called an "all-hazards approach." The scenario the U.S. prepared for was an outbreak of avian flu. However, the counter-measures the government planned and strategies it developed were chosen for their effectiveness against many types of flu, or "all hazards." This turned out to be a very good thing. In 2009, when the swine flu pandemic hit – at a time when not a single one of the top 20 HHS appointees had been confirmed – the Obama administration simply dusted off Bush's 2005 plan and applied it to the situation at hand.

The plan worked, with a few hiccups. The Mexican government and Pan American Health Organization (PAHO) were slow to detect the outbreak in Mexico. Veratect, a firm based thousands of miles away in Seattle, beat both of them to it. Similarly, things went well on the communication front: for the most part, public panic remained low. The largest problem came from Vice President Joe Biden's statement that no one should go in confined areas, which nearly shut down the air travel industry. Interestingly, Biden was relatively new to the execu-tive branch, and had not participated in any previous training. Perhaps the biggest hiccups though were the promises the government left un-filled. In July 2009, they said there'd be 160 million doses of the swine flu vaccine available by the fall. By October, there were only 28 mil-lion doses available, which meant many millions of people were turned away from vaccines.

For the 2010-11 flu season, in contrast, the swine flu strain is now part of the annual flu shot, and vaccinations have been taking place without a hitch. This is good news, and derives in large part from the progress we have made over the past ten years. We must continue our vigilance and commitment to biodefense, while continuing to improve our distribution network. We must be wary of inducing unnecessary hysteria in the public sphere. Bill Maher said that anyone who takes the swine flu vaccine is an "idiot." Glenn Beck said that he would do the opposite of whatever the Secretary of Homeland Security said.   These statements, from the left and the right, make the jobs of preparedness officials harder. Going forward, we need to move away from the notion of partisanship in the era of bioterror. If a bioterror attack were to come, all of us, Republicans and Democrats alike, would be in the same boat.

The Defense We Need

THOMAS DONNELLY

I am very pleased to talk about the report of the Independent Quadrennial Defense Review Panel, which I will summarize shortly. I also want to use the occasion of the panel's report to talk more broadly about the state of the U.S. military, the state of the defense budgets and defense planning, and the politics of the issue, because I think it is a critical moment, particularly for conservatives and Republicans.

I want to pose a question to you: What will it mean for the state of the U.S. armed forces if there is an increase in Republican and conservative representation on Capitol Hill and maybe even some majorities? What will that mean and what should it mean? Let me provide some brief background on the panel. The panel was a creation of the

Thomas Donnelly is Resident Fellow and Director of the Center for Defense Studies at the American Enterprise Institute. Mr. Donnelly gave these remarks at the CSP National Security Group Lunch on 10 September, 2010.

Congress. It is like the QDR in its original conception. There have been numerous defense and strategic reviews since the end of the Cold War. You might ask yourselves, "Why do we do so many of these reviews?" Probably the overriding reason is that nobody ever seems to come up with a durable and satisfactory answer. This is especially true for those concerned about American leadership in the world and the strength of the U.S. armed forces and the need for continued military strength in a very dangerous world. Therefore, there have been QDRs and other kinds of defense reviews, bottom-up reviews, and blue ribbon panels almost since the Berlin Wall came down.

I think it is fair to say that even though the world has changed a lot since then, our ability to anticipate those changes and to answer the fundamental questions about American interests, the use of American power, and the requirements for American power – regardless of what the immediate and present danger may be – has been a difficult and unpleasant task. This was particularly so in the case of the 2010 Quadrennial Defense Review, the one done by the Obama administration. Despite the extraordinary influence and reputation of Secretary Gates – both as a Secretary of War and increasingly now as a Secretary of Defense – in the sense of trying to reshape the institution of the military, there is fairly broad dissatisfaction amongst members of Congress, particularly in the House. Both Ike Skelton and Buck McKeon, current chairman and ranking member of the House Armed Services Committee, reflect a broad, centrist, bipartisan tradition in American politics that views American strength as a necessary condition for a peaceful, prosperous, and stable world. Skelton and McKeon were deeply concerned about the defense cuts that happened right out of the gate in 2009, not so much about those that we now see in prospect from the Obama administration. You may recall that in late 2008 Secretary Gates asked the Joint Chiefs of Staff to look at the defense program and recommend additions that needed to be made; new systems that needed to be purchased or programs that needed to be accelerated. The chiefs came up with about $65 million worth of programmatic add-ons.

Less than six months later, at a time when the stimulus package was being considered and the administration was looking to try to spend its way out of the economic recession, Secretary Gates, among all cabinet agencies and chiefs, was asked to make significant reductions in the defense program. We have seen very substantial and serious program terminations, such as the F-22 fighter, or the cancellations of the Army's Future Combat System and the Zumwalt-class destroyer among other programs. You can go down the list and there have been cancellations, stretch-outs, or further adjustments. Moreover, of course, in a time of war – particularly when American soldiers and Marines are doing back-to-back-to-back combat rotations – the late-in-the-day expansion of the Army and the Marine Corps active duty end strength was capped, and now looks likely to be rolled back. In particular, the burden on the National Guard, the Army National Guard, and the reserve components has remained extraordinarily high. We have mobilized reservists and guardsmen at the rate of more than one hundred thousand per day, every day, since September 11, 2001 up until about three weeks ago. For the first time since 9/11, the number of mobilized reservists has dropped below one hundred thousand, but only barely.

So this was the frame of mind that led to the legislation that established the panel. Again, I would say it reflected a truly bipartisan – or even non-partisan – concern about the state of the U.S. military in the future. Per the usual process of including one nominee or several nominees from all the interested parties, both majority and minority members of the Armed Services Committee, in both bodies, nominated members to the panel. In fact, Secretary Gates was required to nominate the majority of members to the panel. In the end, the panel consisted of twenty members. The panel was co-chaired by Steve Hadley, former National Security Advisor, and Bill Perry, former Secretary of Defense. Other panelists included John Lehman, former Secretary of the Navy, J.D. Crouch, Rudy DeLeon, Eric Edelman, former service chiefs like Dave Jeremiah and former Senator Jim Talent, for whom I worked in the House and who is a fellow at the Heritage Foundation. The result was a disparate group of individuals with a very short timeline to try to turn this report around. The work really only began in April, and the report is still to be published in hardcover.

I want to talk a little bit about the process and about where the panel came out. Again, the process had to be a rapid one, and it consisted of a couple of important steps. The one I was most closely associated with was the effort to try to look ahead to what the 21st century security environment was going to be. Rather than taking this as a prediction of the future, however, or racking and stacking of threats, the approach that we took – I was working under former Marine general Paul Van Riper, who chaired that sub-panel – was to try to establish what the long-term security interests of the United States were. What was not going to change? Obviously, the world was going to change, but did American interests change over the long haul? The consensus of the panel was "no." The United States has always been interested in the "balance of power" in the Asia-Pacific region, or in Europe, or in the Middle East – a term of art that is now expanded to include South Asia and the Indian Ocean as well as the Persian Gulf area. We have always cared about the ability to exploit the "global commons," to use a terrible term of art. In short: the seas, the skies, near-Earth space, and now the realm of cyberspace. These are enduring interests that do not change from Democratic to Republican administrations, that do not change with the decades, and that do not change with the threats. The United States spent a century, an immense amount of blood and treasure, to create what looks like a lasting peace in Europe. That interest is never going to change. Likewise, the United States has been a Pacific power for two centuries. That is never going to change. And we have now been embroiled in the Middle East increasingly for more than a generation. I wish I had invested in a penny stock called CENTCOM in 1979 when it was stood up. If I had pegged my income to the number of Americans in uniform in the CENTCOM AOR, I could have retired a decade ago. And who expects that to change?

That framework set the tone for the panel's recommendations. What the panel essentially said was the following: We cannot afford to retreat in any of these areas. If we continue to make progress in Iraq and Afghanistan and elsewhere in this sort of "Long War" to create a stable Middle East, then we have barely enough forces to do that. In particular, however, we do not have enough power, enough military resources, to respond to the rise of China, to the scramble for power that everybody believes is going to occur around the littoral of the Indian Ocean, and to respond to nuclear proliferation as well as spreading missile capacity across the planet and other threats such as cyber warfare. The panel, being a politically astute collection of individuals, came very rapidly to that conclusion. The members of the panel were looking for a way to express that in a way that would be understood by the political class and in a Washington context. What the panel came up with was the idea that we should go back to the force levels that were established originally in the Clinton administration under Secretary of Defense Les Aspin, who did the very first of these post-Cold War reviews, called the "Bottom-Up Review." If you compare where we are now and what a Democratic administration thought at the beginning of the peaceful and prosperous decade of the 1990s was the minimum requirement for American power, and you just lay the force structure today against that force structure, it is significantly smaller now than it was then. In the most graphic measure, the size of the United States Navy – which as late as the end of the Bush administration was more than five hundred ships, and was programmed to shrink to three hundred and fifty ships under the Bottom-Up Review – is now at about two hundred and eighty ships. The Navy is extremely hard-pressed and is highly unlikely to be able to sustain those force levels going forward. If you think of what the security environment is going to be in the most contentious areas of the world and, in particular, in the Asia-Pacific where the world's most rapidly growing economies and most rapidly growing militaries are, this is a recipe for retreat of American power that none of the panel members found acceptable. In this regard the report, in summary, is as much a political effort as it is an analytical effort. We did not have the staff capacity or the analytic capacity to do what is necessary to do; the kinds of trade-offs and analyses that would produce a more robust number. But as a mark on the wall it is a good place to start. It will, I hope, provoke a conversation that needs to happen going forward.

I would conclude by saying, particularly for the Republican Party and a conservative movement that quite rightly feels itself on the march and with every prospect of success in November, that the political energy is very much coming from absolute concern and distress over the policies of the Obama administration. In particular the fiscal condition in which our government and our nation finds itself. It would be a tragedy, indeed an abandonment of conservative principles, if America shrunk from its global role. This is not about the size but about the role of government. What is the purview of government and what is not the purview of government?

We should remember that as the Declaration of Independence says, our first right is the right to life. That is, to security. Even before political liberty or prosperity, we must be safe. There needs to be a secure place for American freedoms to prosper and for Americans to prosper and grow. As we go forward, as we look to an opportunity not only to criticize what the government does, but to shape what the government does after November, we need to not approach that moment as accountants; not simply as those who need to staunch the flow of red ink. We also need to preserve the power that is necessary for our prosperity. It is impossible to think of a global economic recovery without American global security guarantees to ensure the free flow and the cheap flow of trade. As we go forward, we should look back. We should ask ourselves, as always, "what would Ronald Reagan do?" Ronald Reagan always put the security of the nation above balancing the budget or limiting the size of government.

As someone who certainly prefers the GDP metric to other indicators, it is important to consider it in the following way. It is important to underscore where the money is really going, and it is important to compare apples to apples over time. The important question is the question of affordability. There is an approach that says, "Everybody has got to pony up to getting the government's books in order and so everybody has got to feel the pain." First of all, the arithmetic does not come close to adding up. You could eliminate the Pentagon entirely and the federal deficit for this year would not even be halved. So, if you are going to be serious about putting the fiscal house in order, you should be like Willie Sutton and go where the money is. And it is not really in the Defense Department. Even while we are fighting two wars in Iraq and Afghanistan, we are still spending less than a nickel of our annual wealth on military power.

So, if you ask yourself, "is America in decline? Can we afford the burdens we are asked to bear?" The answer is unquestionably "no" and "yes," respectively. We get an immense return on a miniscule investment from our military. That is the only way in which I think those numbers are important. Otherwise, you get Democrats out there who

The question is, "Can we afford what we need to do?" And

the answer is, quite obviously, "absolutely yes."

will say that we spend much more on defense than the next eighteen countries combined – all those kinds of silly metrics that go on. That is not the important thing. The question is, "Can we afford what we need to do?" And the answer is, quite obviously, "absolutely yes." Again, we are quite right to be concerned about the profligate spending of government. But the idea that you can solve these fiscal problems by making defense cuts is bad arithmetic.

I would not say that our commitments have really increased. I would calculate commitments in a larger way than just counting the number of operations or the number of folks deployed. Let us compare twenty years ago to today. Twenty years ago, we had three hundred thousand or three hundred fifty thousand people in Germany and deployed across Europe at the height of the Cold War. We had an immense fleet of aircraft carriers and submarines that patrolled the Atlantic, tracking Soviet submarines and so forth. We also had a presence in East Asia that included a hundred thousand deployed forces with bases in the Philippines, Japan, and other places. We also had commitments in Korea, with larger deployments there than we have today. Prior to 1979, there were very few Americans in the Persian Gulf region. Since then, hemlines have gone up and down across the planet.

Today, the size of the U.S. military, however, is two-thirds the size that it was twenty years ago. On modernization, by all other measures of combat effectiveness, even on a per capita basis, at best we have held our own. All that happened while our commitment in Europe has decreased significantly. Last, our commitment in East Asia, our presence in East Asia, is far less than it used to be. However, our presence across the Islamic world, or the Greater Middle East, has increased, of course. So, the net effect has been an overall decrease. If you calculate it as a slice of our wealth that portion has likewise diminished. Obviously, there are a lot of risks and dangers out there, but nothing approaches the level of existential danger once posed by the Soviet Union – at least in the sense of being able to snuff us out tomorrow. Even though the Russian arsenal is still there, I am not saying it is not a dangerous world. To me, however, that looks like getting more for less overall. I would not begin to tell this to a guy wearing a desert combat uniform for a second. Looking at it from fifty thousand feet, however, we get a lot for a little and the world is overall a better place. Again, we do not face that same kind of threat of complete elimination as a nation, as a civilization, that we faced for fifty years of standoff with the Soviets.

The Danger of EMP

PETER PRY

T hank you for the opportunity to speak about the EMP threat. By way of background, I am President of EMPact America, a grassroots organization trying to mobilize citizens, communities, and the state and federal governments to protect our nation from the clear and present danger of an EMP event.

An electromagnetic pulse can be caused in two ways. A nuclear weapon detonates high above the atmosphere, above an altitude of forty kilometers, and interacts with the upper atmosphere, causing what is basically a super-energetic radio wave which is harmless to people directly. It'll pass right through your body and you won't even know it.

Dr. Peter Vincent Pry is President of EMPact America, Director of the U.S. Nuclear Strategy Forum, and served on the staffs of the Central Intelligence Agency, the House Armed Services Committee, the EMP Commission, and the Strategic Posture Commission. Dr. Pry gave these remarks at the CSP National Security Group Lunch on 8 October, 2010.

But it will destroy electronic systems across vast regions of the earth's surface. If the weapon is detonated, even at that low altitude for example, you'd be taking out the New England states, all of New York and probably half of Pennsylvania. If you detonated at higher altitude, you can cover the entire United States, parts of Canada and Mexico and fry electronics across that whole region.

There's another threat, a natural threat, from geomagnetic storms. These routinely occur in countries of high northern latitudes. They rarely come down and affect the United States. There was one in 1989 that knocked out the electric grid in Quebec. But we now know, as a result of the work of the EMP Commission, that there is a phenomenon known as a "great geomagnetic storm" that occurs perhaps every century or so. The last time was the Carrington Event in 1859. This is caused when a solar flare, technically known as a coronal mass ejection, comes out of the sun and strikes the earth's magnetosphere. And this causes an EMP very similar to that of a very high-yield, multi-megaton, nuclear weapon. The effects are very similar too, in that they would take out long lines, power lines, telecommunications systems – anything that has a large dimension that the pulse can couple into. And both of these things can basically end civilization as we know it, because we cannot exist as a modern society without electronics, particularly the electric power grid. That is the keystone infrastructure. Everything ultimately depends upon electric power – communications, transportation, banking and finance, food and water.

We have built cities in locations today where people wouldn't have been able to in the past, because electric power enables us to pump water there to sustain those cities. And when the electric power grid goes, all of those infrastructures that support our society go with it. Within hours or days of the electromagnetic pulse, it wouldn't be like a normal blackout. We can recover from normal blackouts pretty quickly, but an EMP is likely to do things like destroy the big transformers. There are, for example, about three hundred big transformers that are absolutely indispensable to the operation of the electric power grid. They aren't even made in this country anymore, ironically. The United States invented the electric power grid, but we don't even make the basic components here anymore. There are only two nations in the world that make these big transformers for export purposes. It

There's really no excuse for the United States to continue to be vulnerable to EMP. We have technological solutions. They're inexpensive to implement. The Commission came up with a plan. It worked eight years on a plan that is in the coffer, that Congress has and that could be implemented.

takes eighteen months to build one transformer, and we have almost no spares. What would happen if you couldn't restore electric power in this country for eighteen months? Well, the Commission estimates that within twelve months – given our current state of unpreparedness – we would lose most of our population. Estimates indicate that anywhere from two thirds to ninety percent of the American people would perish from a single nuclear weapon. One. Detonated at high altitude, that had those kinds of effects on the power grid. Or from a single great geomagnetic storm, which occur every hundred years or so. They're inevitable. Most scientists think that we're overdue for one of these since the last one occurred in 1859. We know when they occurred, even though in 1859, for example, they didn't know what was happening. But there are clear signs. You can go back in the historical record. People notice when the aurora borealis shows up on the equator – it's bright as day. Because the aurora borealis is so intense, people record those in their diaries.

So we go back every century or so. You can do the math. 1859. It's 2010 now. When's the next one? The next peak solar cycle is in 2012, 2013. So we could be very close to another great geomagnetic storm.

I never wanted to be "Mr. EMP". I've been working this issue since 1985 when I started working at the CIA and then came over to Congress and served on the EMP Commission and was involved in hearings and all the rest. But when I first started working this issue on the Hill, I thought, "Wow, this is such a common sense kind of a threat." And the solution is actually ready at hand, unlike most other threats, like an all-out nuclear war, or a terrorist bomb smuggled into a port, or biological terrorism. We'll never really be completely safe against those things. There's always going to be a race between our security and the threat that the enemy can come up with. But there's really no excuse for the United States to continue to be vulnerable to EMP. We have technological solutions. They're inexpensive to implement. The Commission came up with a plan. It worked eight years on a plan that is in the coffer, that Congress has and that could be implemented. And it wouldn't even be that expensive.

Those three hundred big transformers? For two hundred million dollars, you could protect those big transformers. Not much of a price to pay to save two thirds of the American population, right? And you would think – I thought, when I started working this problem – that, okay, we'll do a bill and we'll have the solution within a year. Well, here it is, I mean, it's almost fifteen years later since I started working on this particular issue. We are so close to a solution.

The biggest part of the problem is not technological. The thing that's going to get us killed is our own strategic culture – it's the law that's going to get us killed. Everybody is arguing over who has jurisdiction and responsibility for protecting against EMP. The Department of Homeland Security said, "Well, it's a nuclear threat, so it's DOD's responsibility." And the Department of Defense says, "Well, it's protecting the civilian electric power grid. That's a DHS responsibility." And believe it or not, they say you never should see how laws and sausages are made. But that's been the problem.

Now, we came very close in 2010.There was a bill that finally got passed through the House: HR-5026, The Grid Reliability and Infrastructure Defense Act. The bill passed unanimously on a bipartisan basis. How many things get passed on a bipartisan basis these days in this political climate? That's how strong the evidence was from not just the EMP Commission, but there were several other commissions, including the National Academy of Sciences that had independently looked at this and said, "Yeah, this is really a threat. We got to do something." So the bill went forward to the Senate and we hoped it would sail through the Senate, but guess what? It didn't. It shipwrecked again, on this question about who really has administrative responsibility for this? Legally, for this? Anyway, we have powerful allies in the Senate, including Senator Reid. There's bipartisan support for this. And those of us supporting the bill have been promised that it will be brought up for a vote in the lame duck. So there's still a chance it can pass. We're that close. If that bill passes, it's going to be implementing one of the major recommendations of the EMP Commission. It will put in place, for the first time, the legal authorities and the financial mechanisms so we can get this country protected against EMP. If we had five years and ten or twenty billion dollars, we could basically forget about this threat and go worry about other things, because this is a threat that we can protect the critical civilian infrastructures against. It's something we can do something about. And I wish, those of you who are working in Congress, those of you who are on staff, I wish I were in your shoes. Because you're probably where you are because you want to make a difference with your life. And I'm doing this because I want to make a difference with my life. And this is one of those few areas where, with just a little effort, if you can get one bill passed, you can make a huge difference. You can protect, save, two thirds of the American people. We can take away probably the main reason Iran is working on the bomb, because it only needs one bomb. That answers the mystery about why countries like North Korea and Iran have nuclear programs. They'll have crude nuclear missiles, crude nuclear warheads, perhaps only a few of them. Why would they do that? We've got thousands of nuclear weapons. They only need one.

China's Military Rising

PETER BROOKES

G ood afternoon. It's a pleasure to be with you.

China seems to be on everybody's mind these days and rightfully so. But it's not just economics and trade that people are thinking about, it's China's military as well.

Quite frankly, China is involved in an unprecedented military buildup. This has been going on for quite some time now, and it's taking place across the board of Chinese military capabilities.

You can read about it in the Pentagon's annual report to Congress on Chinese military power. Once again, this year, they've given a fair

Peter Brookes is a Heritage Foundation Senior Fellow for National Security Affairs and a former Deputy Assistant Secretary of Defense. Mr. Brookes gave these remarks at the CSP National Security Group Lunch on 8 October, 2010.

treatment to the subject, despite the challenges of getting the document through the interagency process and into the public domain.

But remember it's not telling you everything as it is an unclassified report and there are reasons things are said—and not said—in that report.

However, it's still a pretty good primer, as it has been over the years, about China's strategy and their military capabilities. Like I said, it's very careful in its wording and you have to read between the lines sometimes, but it's definitely worth a look if you're interested in this topic.

And the rise of the People's Liberation Army, the collective name for China's armed forces, is certainly an issue worth considering here today, for China's military modernization has been getting scant attention in comparison to the challenges of terrorism and the wars in Iraq and Afghanistan—and understandably so.

But it would be a mistake to dismiss what is happening in China, especially since it's unclear exactly what China's strategic intentions and ambitions are. While not everyone is in agreement, I personally believe that China has grand ambitions, even aspiring to replace the United States at the head of the table of state powers.

Not surprisingly, the Chinese are very coy about this matter. And if you look at their writings on this issue, they will talk about being careful about letting others know exactly what their ambitions are so as to minimize suspicion about China's rise in the international system.

But for a number of reasons, I think we have good reason to be concerned about China's rise, especially from a security perspective. An area that is particularly noteworthy is the development of China's power projection forces, which will allow Beijing to extend its influence well beyond its periphery. For instance, there has been a lot of emphasis on the Chinese navy, air force and missile programs.

In fact, most people don't realize this, but China now has the second largest navy in Asia, if you include the United States. China has new destroyers with advanced missiles. An indigenous aircraft carrier, which many people said would never happen, is actually coming to pass. In fact, we may see a Chinese aircraft carrier at sea in the next couple of years.

If the Chinese can access U.S. cyber and space systems in a significant way, Beijing could theoretically win a war against us without firing a shot.

People have long said that carrier-based air operations were just too hard for the Chinese to ever do. They were so far behind the United States that they would never attempt to join the ranks of carrier navies. In fact, I heard that personally from some of our own military and intelligence leaders over the years.

As it looks, we will not be the only country with an aircraft carrier in the Pacific in the years to come. The Chinese are also building nuclear attack submarines and fleet ballistic missile submarines—what we call SSBNs. More on this a little later.

The army, which has been large, is actually downsizing. But they're professionalizing as they reduce their numbers. They're doing things that we've done for years, such as developing a professional non-commissioned officer corps.

As anybody who has served in the armed forces knows, the NCO corps is the backbone of the modern military. So they're moving in that direction, which will improve the fighting effectiveness of PLA land forces in the years to come.

The PLA Air Force is developing long-range surface to air missiles—or SAMs. They have fourth-generation fighter aircraft now, which is not quite on par with what we have, but they're closing the capabilities gap.

We're not talking about the Chinese having the capability of the Joint Strike Fighter, but they're not too far behind some of our current systems that are still very capable in their own right.

They're also working on joint operations among the different services, which will increase the efficiency and lethality of the Chinese PLA.

As part of China's asymmetric military strategy, the PLA is developing counter-space and cyber capabilities, too. The Chinese believe that by using asymmetric capabilities – in other words, taking what they perceive to be their strength versus what they perceive to be our weakness –they can get into a David versus Goliath situation with us, where a smaller David, being China, can defeat more powerful Goliath, being the United States.

This is an important part of their current military strategy. If the Chinese can access U.S. cyber and space systems in a significant way, Beijing could theoretically win a war against us without firing a shot.

But one of the areas that is getting the least attention within the debate on China's military buildup is their strategic forces, known as the Second Artillery, especially in the context of our consideration of the New Strategic Arms Reduction Treaty (New START) with Russia.

Even with the debate on the Hill and elsewhere on START – verification procedures, the 20 to 30 percent decrease in our strategic forces, the restraints on missile defense, and so on—the fact that China is building up its strategic forces does not seem to be considered to a great extent.

Of course, there were obviously deliberations that I certainly wasn't privileged to, but the fact of the matter is, in my view: as we're building down, China is building up.

And there are reasons to be worried about this.

The Pentagon in its report, for instance, writes that China has the most active land-based ballistic and cruise missile programs in the world today. They have new missiles. They have new missile units. They are upgrading existing strategic systems. They're working on countermeasures to ballistic missile defense, including an array of penetration aids. A lot is going on.

And while China is building and modernizing, we're not. For instance, I think most of the B-52 strategic bombers we fly today average about 32 years of age and, in many cases, those planes are older than the pilots that fly them.

Originally, China had a limited number of liquid-fueled fixed silo ICBMs armed with 3-5 megaton weapons. Today, China is moving

If there's any country out there that could rush to nuclear parity with the United States and Russia, it's China. The Chinese have the capability, and based on double-digit increases in their defense budgets in recent tears, they're clearly willing to lavish largesse on the PLA, including the Second Artillery.

beyond those fixed silos to road-mobile solid-fueled ICBMs, increasing the responsiveness and survivability of its nuclear force.

Along the same lines, it's been reported that China's Second Artillery (i.e., nuclear forces) have built 3,000 miles of underground tunnels, called the "Underground Great Wall," likely for their road-mobile ICBM force, improving their deterrence and counterstrike capabilities. It'll also keep us from knowing how many road mobile missiles they have put into service.

Beyond this, China is moving from a strategic monad to an expanded nuclear triad. As I mentioned they now have new SSBNs such as the Jin class—or Type 094—which will carry twelve intercontinental-range submarine-launched ballistic missiles (SLBMs). It is expected that China will build at least five of that class.

They're already working on the next class of SSBN, which is going to be the Type 096. And it's going to carry as many as 24 SLBMs. This development is significant, because submarines are probably the most survivable element of a nuclear triad.

For the third leg of the triad, the Chinese are developing their air arm. They have the B-6 bomber, which is basically an upgraded TU-16 Badger from the Soviet days. In addition, they're developing air-launched land attack cruise missiles for the B-6.

It's not clear whether these cruise missiles would carry conventional or nuclear warheads, but some analysts believe they will be nuclear capable.

The Pentagon also says that China has MIRV capabilities, which means they may be able to put a number of warheads on a single ballistic missile. As such, we may not have a good sense of how many warheads China has in their strategic forces.

Some put the number at 250 warheads. Others say the number is two times larger than that. With a MIRV capability and the new SSBNs coming on-line, the number of warheads could add up pretty quickly beyond the currently estimated baseline.

As such, in my view, if there's any country out there that could rush to nuclear parity with the United States and Russia, it's China. The Chinese have the capability, and based on double-digit increases in their defense budgets in recent tears, they're clearly willing to lavish largesse on the PLA, including the Second Artillery.

Another thing that worries me is Chinese nuclear policy. It's critically important when you're thinking about threats that you not only look at capabilities, but look at intent as well. It can take years to build capabilities. Intent can change overnight. And that's really the critical thing here.

China is difficult to understand at times. They keep their strategic cards very close to their chest. It's hard to discern exactly what they're thinking about things; they're not transparent about security issues.

But we have believed for some time that China's nuclear policy is based on two concepts: no first use and a minimum deterrence. But I'm hearing from people who follow this matter that there is an ongoing debate in China about their nuclear forces and policy, especially among young Chinese strategists.

So, there's a question about China's minimum deterrence policy, which is basically the ability to undertake a retaliatory strike against counter-value forces – that is, against an enemy's major population centers. Basically, if you take a shot at us, we have the capability to retaliate by holding your people at risk.

Now, the question is whether China is moving from minimum deterrence to limited deterrence structure. In fact, the Pentagon, interestingly, already calls China's nuclear policy a limited deterrent strategy, which, if we agree on definitions, means they have the ability not only to conduct a second strike against counter-value targets, but also go against an opponent's offensive nuclear forces in some fashion. That means you would have to have more delivery vehicles as well as more warheads than necessary for a minimum deterrence posture.

There's also discussion among analysts that while China has an active defense strategy, this strategy may allow for preemption. In fact, China's "active defense" policy is actually very offensive in nature if you look at some of the wars they've been involved in since 1969. But notably, they've always called these offensive-looking actions "defensive," such as in their war in 1979 with Vietnam, which China initiated. China was the aggressor, but called it a defensive action.

As such, there are also questions about the policy of preemption today in China's nuclear forces, especially as their strategic forces grow in size and capability. Could China at some point transition from a second-strike to a first-strike policy? The problem is we just don't know. China is very secretive about its nuclear policy.

In fact, the Pentagon has been trying to have exchanges with the PLA on nuclear matters, but so far they've kept us at arm's length. And because they've refused to engage substantively on the nuclear issue, our knowledge may be more limited than before, especially in light of the evolution of their strategic forces.

As such, I think that it's really pretty important that as we look at START – which is a treaty with Russia that will last at least ten years – we also look at the issue of China's military, especially developments in the Second Artillery.

China is a rising power that is becoming a peer competitor of the United States, which may hope to ultimately eclipse the United States as the preeminent power in the Pacific—and even globally.

And perhaps most troubling is that some PLA writings identify that United States as China's most likely enemy—a view that should leave us very concerned and attentive to developments across the Pacific in China.

Continuing to underestimate China in the future or not to pay enough attention to security developments there could have dire consequences.

U.S.-Pakistan Relations

LISA CURTIS

I am here to talk about Pakistan, a country that today poses some of the most serious foreign policy and national security challenges to the United States. Indeed, the tribal border areas between Pakistan and Afghanistan constitute the most dangerous terrorist safe haven in the world. The increase in the tempo of drone strikes in this area – which is only nominally controlled by Pakistan – over the last year and half has helped to diminish the threat considerably. The drones have made it more difficult for al-Qaeda to plot, train, and organize their ranks, which have been shaken by the relentless missile campaign. The Obama administration deserves credit for its willingness to engage in this aggressive drone strategy.

Lisa Curtis is Senior Research Fellow in the Asian Studies Center at the Heritage Foundation. She previously served on the professional staff of the Senate Foreign Relations Committee and as the White-House appointed senior adviser to the Assistant Secretary of State for South Asian Affairs. Ms. Curtis gave these remarks at the CSP National Security Group Lunch on 10 September, 2010.

That said, the threat of international terrorism emanating from Pakistan is still very high. There is a plethora of Islamist extremist organizations in addition to al-Qaeda that reside in Pakistan's Federally Administered Tribal Areas (FATA). These include the Afghan Taliban (which fight coalition forces in Afghanistan), the Pakistani Taliban (which directed the Times Square bombing attempt last May), the Lashkar-e-Tayyiba (which carried out the November 2008 Mumbai attacks), the Jaish-e-Mohammed (which was behind the 2002 murder and kidnapping of *Wall Street Journal* reporter Daniel Pearl), and the Jalaluddin Haqqani network (responsible for some of the fiercest attacks on U.S. forces in Afghanistan). While these groups are not card-carrying al-Qaeda members, they subscribe to a similar anti-West pan-Islamist ideology. They also facilitate al-Qaeda activities by helping with logistics, training, and providing safe passage and hiding to al-Qaeda operatives.

Over the last eighteen months Pakistan has shown greater commitment to confronting the militant groups that threaten the Pakistani state. The Pakistani military cracked down on pro-Taliban militants in the Swat Valley last summer, causing most of the militants to flee and allowing normalcy to return to the region. The pro-Taliban militants had sought to establish their own mini-state by overtaking the local administration and implementing Shariah law. The Swat Valley military operation has helped improve Pakistani stability and restore greater confidence among the Pakistani people that the Army will stand up to the militants to protect their civil rights.

Although Pakistan is moving in the right direction with regard to fighting terrorists that target the Pakistani state, Islamabad continues to hedge on its support for the Afghan Taliban and related militants, like the Jalaluddin Haqqani network. Rather than viewing the various groups as connected and thus posing an existential threat to the country—which is how the U.S. views the situation – most Pakistani military strategists are more worried about India trying to encircle Pakistan by gaining influence in Afghanistan. They calculate that the Taliban and Haqqani network offer the best chance for countering India's regional influence.

Still, given the enormous challenges Pakistan faces, especially now with the flood crisis, the U.S. finds it necessary to calibrate how far it pushes Islamabad to take on the various militant groups. Years of support from the Pakistani security establishment to these groups have made it extremely difficult to obtain a unified and determined position from the Army on moving against them in a comprehensive manner. The Army and intelligence agencies, by feeding a narrative to the Pakistani people that supported the militant groups, has in some ways undermined its own ability to maintain the writ of the state.

The recent Pakistani intelligence report indicating that internal militancy constituted an existential threat to Pakistan demonstrates that the security establishment is beginning to recognize the inherent risks of providing a permissive environment for militant groups of any stripe. It is not clear, however, that this view represents a permanent change of attitude or has been widely accepted at all levels of the military establishment. The view has reportedly gained some traction among top leaders, like Chief of Army Staff General Ashfaq Kayani and head of the Inter-Service Intelligence directorate (ISI) Shuja Pasha. However, the notion that internal militants could pose more of a threat to Pakistan than India is certainly not a view that has filtered down through the ranks of the military. Nonetheless, the fact that the report surfaced at all is slightly encouraging.

Another obstacle to gaining Pakistan's full cooperation against the Afghan Taliban and related militant groups is President Obama's pledge to begin withdrawing U.S. forces from Afghanistan in July 2011 – a point he unfortunately reiterated during a speech from the oval office ten days ago. It is difficult to overstate the damage the timeline has done to the U.S. Afghan strategy and, in particular, Washington's efforts to partner with Islamabad. Pakistani officials who calculate the U.S. is pulling up stakes in Afghanistan next year are loathe to break ties to the Taliban, on whom they would have to rely in the event of a premature U.S. withdrawal from the region. Pakistani military officials argue: "Why should we let go of something that has helped serve our own national security when the Americans are going to be gone in a year anyway?"

I also want to caution against buying into the Obama administration argument that it has made tremendous strides with Pakistan as compared to the previous Bush administration. This simply is not the case. The U.S. faces the same challenges with Pakistan today that it faced during the Bush administration. The Obama administration often points to the Swat Valley military operation as vindication of its Pakistan policy. But the motivation to take on the militants in Swat came from the Pakistanis themselves and did not appear to be driven by any initiative from the Obama administration.

Secondly, it was the Bush administration that shepherded the transition to democracy in Pakistan in 2007-2008. The February 2008 elections that brought to power the civilian government led by Pakistan People's Party President Asif Ali Zardari and led to Musharraf finally stepping down from power in August 2008 occurred on George Bush's watch.

Now, I will give credit to Obama administration officials for continually highlighting that the militant groups located in Pakistan pose a threat to the stability of the state. I would argue, however, that they must go further. U.S. officials must push back on Pakistani calls for the U.S. to limit Indian influence in Afghanistan.

India supports the U.S. goal of preventing the Taliban from regaining influence. There is simply no moral or strategic case to be made in favor of alienating a fellow democracy that supports U.S. objectives in the region to placate a country that continues to harbor our enemies.

Instead, U.S. officials must convince the Pakistani leadership that focusing on building up their own economy and their own human capital base is the best way to shore up their regional position. If Pakistan is worried about India's emerging global status, it should focus on catching up by dealing with its internal problems, rather than supporting militant groups in order to needle India. Again, I reiterate that only by demonstrating our own commitment to stabilizing Afghanistan will we convince the Pakistanis to demobilize the Taliban and see the benefits of normalizing ties to India.

Some U.S. officials argue that we must accept a certain amount of ambiguity in the Pakistan military's attitudes and actions toward militancy since the links between the security services and militant groups have been built up over a period of several years. But the

The U.S. needs to convince Pakistan that cases against terrorists who attack India should be treated no differently than cases against terrorists who act in other parts of the world. By treating terrorists focused on India with kid gloves, Islamabad has created a permissive environment for terrorists to operate more generally.

Obama administration must distinguish between Pakistani strategy and a genuine struggle to dismantle the various militant groups.

FLOOD CRISIS

Let me turn to the floods, because this is an enormous event in Pakistan and there's a real possibility of increased lawlessness and greater political instability arising out of the crisis. Even though the number of lives lost in the flooding – about 1,600 – pales in comparison to the casualties from the 2005 earthquake – about 70,000 – the extent of the damage from the floods is far more expansive and the suffering of the affected population will likely last longer.

Close to 60,000 square miles of territory was flooded and over one million homes were destroyed. Nine million acres of crops were destroyed, which raises the prospect of food shortages and price hikes.

The U.S. government has responded robustly to the crisis and has been the largest single donor providing over $250 million in aid and crucial helicopter assistance. U.S. private donations are lagging, though, at about $25 million five weeks into the crisis. This compares to over $1 billion in private donations for Haiti earthquake relief.

This is only the latest crisis Pakistan has suffered and adds another layer of uncertainty to the country's future. In addition to the floods, Pakistan has been wracked by ethnic/political violence in Karachi. Moreover, in just the last ten days, over 100 Pakistanis have been killed in a wave of terrorist attacks.

Once the immediate flood crisis subsides, the U.S. will need to continue to focus on helping Pakistan rebuild flood-devastated infrastructure and cope with the longer-term economic challenges from the disaster. The U.N. has estimated that it will take billions in international assistance to rehabilitate the affected areas. Portions of the Kerry-Lugar funding should be re-programmed and even expedited, if necessary, to rebuild the flood-devastated areas of the country.

U.S. POLICY MOVING FORWARD

So how does U.S. policy take into account the myriad challenges to Pakistani stability and the acute need for Pakistani cooperation in the U.S.-led mission to stabilize Afghanistan? We need to continue to shore up the civilian population and encourage political stability by helping in the flood reconstruction and moving forward with civilian assistance authorized in the Kerry/Lugar aid legislation signed into law last year.

At the same time, the U.S. must carefully calibrate and condition its assistance to the Pakistani military. This is complicated, though, since we need to bolster the Pakistani military's fight against the militants. It is nearly impossible to develop an effective policy toward a military that is helping us at the tactical level while hurting us at the strategic level. We receive crucial counterterrorism cooperation from Pakistan that has provided U.S. authorities with access to high value detainees and information that has helped thwart terrorist strikes. The cooperation is uneven, however, and there are numerous indications that the Pakistani military leadership is not taking sufficient action to shut down the Taliban's sanctuary and other terrorist groups like the Lashkar-e-Tayyiba.

Another point of leverage for the U.S. is to raise public awareness about Pakistani involvement with terrorism. This is essentially what happened when U.S. officials briefed the press about Pakistan's involvement in the bombing of the Indian embassy in Kabul in July 2008. U.S. officials, on the other hand, have been tight-lipped about revelations from the David Headley investigations on Pakistan's role in the Mumbai attacks. Although the Indians claim Headley revealed there was direct Pakistani intelligence involvement in those attacks,

U.S. officials have remained silent on the issue.

We must work to get a better handle on the extremist threat inside Pakistan. The Pakistani authorities need to demonstrate their willingness to punish any citizens that incite, support, or otherwise abet terrorism anywhere in the world. The U.S. needs to convince Pakistan that cases against terrorists who attack India should be treated no differently than cases against terrorists who act in other parts of the world. By treating terrorists focused on India with kid gloves, Islamabad has created a permissive environment for terrorists to operate more generally, especially since many of the various terrorist groups share a pan-Islamist ideology and provide each other with tactical cooperation and logistical support. By trying to support dual policies on terrorism, the Pakistanis put themselves at a disadvantage. We need to keep driving this point home.

INDIA-PAKISTAN RELATIONS

Part of stabilizing Afghanistan and overcoming the terrorist threat in Pakistan involves encouraging India and Pakistan to develop a different paradigm for their relationship. This new paradigm should be based on economic integration and trade and efforts to enhance regional security by jointly confronting non-state actors. The India-Pakistan dialogue is continuing but has made little progress since it was re-started earlier this year. Pakistan's failure to prosecute the seven Lashkar-e-Tayyiba members it arrested a year ago appears to be the major stumbling block to progress.

The civilian leaders in Pakistan are currently helping to move the Indo-Pakistani dialogue forward. Their hands are often tied by the military, but they persist in finding ways to convince their military counterparts on the advantages of dialogue. I raise this point because I think there is often a temptation in Washington to believe that it might be easier to deal with a military government. But we should consider that the civilians, by and large, have a moderating influence on Pakistani decision making with regard to India.

SAFETY OF NUCLEAR WEAPONS

The argument that things can get worse in Pakistan is a compelling one. Although there is no immediate danger of the nuclear weapons arsenal falling into the hands of terrorists, this is a nightmare scenario that U.S. policymakers must consider.

The concern regarding the nuclear weapons is not that the Taliban will attack a facility, take it over, and then have their finger on the nuclear button. The real danger is more insidious. The concern is that gradually terrorists will gain access to individuals in charge of the nuclear programs or will be able to obtain information on nuclear programs through their links to the security establishment. Indeed, former CIA Director George Tenet's memoirs detail an incident that occurred in August 2001 in which two former Pakistani nuclear scientists met with Usama bin-Laden and al-Zawahiri. The U.S. went directly to former President Musharraf with the information and prevailed on him to take action against the individuals.

This 2001 incident prompted the U.S. to begin a program of cooperation with Pakistan on nuclear safety and security issues. Following the incident, the U.S. realized it had to acknowledge the reality of the Pakistan nuclear weapons program and to take pragmatic steps to help the Pakistan government protect its nuclear assets from non-state actors.

New Days, Old Ways

DAVID J. TRACHTENBERG

A review of
*The New Nobility: The Restoration of Russia's Security State
and the Enduring Legacy of the KGB*
by Andrei Soldatov and Irina Borogan

2010 PublicAffairs, a member of the Perseus Books Group

Historians may characterize the post-Cold War history of Russia as a period of unrealized expectations. The strategic partnership with the West that was envisioned after the fall of the Soviet Union has remained elusive. The initial high hopes that Russia would shake off the authoritarian traits of the Soviet era and grow strong democratic roots appear to be evaporating. Nowhere is there more striking evidence of this than in the evolution of Russia's state security services.

In Soviet times, the Committee on State Security, known by its Russian acronym KGB, was perhaps the most feared institution in

David J. Trachtenberg is President and CEO of Shortwaver Consulting, LLC. He served as Principal Deputy Assistant Secretary of Defense from 2001-2003 and as senior Professional Staff Member on the House Armed Services Committee from 1995-2001.

Soviet society. As an instrument of internal repression and control, the KGB was notorious for its often ruthless enforcement of the Soviet state's dictatorial rule. As an institution, it was seemingly omnipresent and omnipotent, with its officers enjoying the perks of power and privilege. Its actions remained beyond the reach of public accountability.

Even after the demise of the Soviet Union, it is no easy task to lift the curtain of secrecy that has veiled the activities of the Federal Security Service (FSB), the post-KGB security apparatus within Russia. But in "The New Nobility: The Restoration of Russia's Security State and the Enduring Legacy of the KGB," Russian authors Andrei Soldatov and Irina Borogan present a gripping and well-documented narrative of how Russia's security services evolved after the collapse of the Soviet Union and how they have regained their elite status thanks in no small measure to the support of one of their former leaders, the current Prime Minister and former President of Russia Vladimir Putin.

The title of the book is taken from a speech by Nikolai Patrushev, Putin's successor as head of the FSB, in which he stated that the officers of the FSB had become Russia's "new nobility." Indeed, the authors explain that Russia's security services see themselves as Russia's "saviors" and the "only forces capable of saving the country from internal and external enemies." Importantly, they note: "Rather than a revival of the Soviet KGB, the FSB had evolved into something more powerful and more frightening, an agency whose scope, under the aegis of a veteran KGB officer, extended well beyond the bounds of its predecessor."

These are strong words. But Soldatov and Borogan are well-qualified to draw such a conclusion. For many years they have been shedding light on the darkest corners of Russia's state security services. Their findings have been published online and in various newspapers. Being an investigative journalist in Russia can be hazardous to one's health – there have been at least 18 unsolved cases of murdered journalists in the past decade – and the authors have had their share of unpleasant encounters with the FSB. Yet their ability to uncover inconvenient truths in a country that is not known for its appreciation of a free press is remarkable. Through their determined efforts they have produced a chronicle that is detailed and well-written. It is also

"There is a sense of déjà vu: the practice of surveillance of dissidents is back, taking people off trains, preventing conversations. The practice not only returned, but is enriched with new means of pressure on the people."

unsettling for those who hoped Russia would develop democratic institutions and a society governed by the rule of law.

The book documents the resurgent influence of the FSB in virtually all aspects of Russian life – from the activities of sports clubs and businesses to the tracking and "elimination" of so-called "extremists" who pose a threat to the Russian state. The authors note that the surveillance practices employed by the FSB are not as widespread as those used by the KGB; but they state ominously that "Russia's measures to closely monitor the lives of its citizens reflect an authoritarian hand – one less interested in the goals of civil society and more concerned with maintaining rigid control."

The authors provide a rich context for understanding the recent trend toward authoritarianism in contemporary Russia. Readers unfamiliar with the internal workings of authoritarian regimes may be surprised by the seemingly paranoid Russian focus on internal security. Those, however, who have studied Russian and Soviet history will not be surprised by the mindset reflected in the statement of an FSB directorate chief that "'internal sedition' has always been more terrible for Russia than any military invasion." The enduring nature of this mindset may help explain the growth of the FSB's domestic surveillance activities under Putin. This growth has continued to the present day, prompting Lyudmilla Alekseeva, the Moscow head of the Helsinki Group, to declare: "There is a sense of déjà vu: the practice of surveillance of dissidents is back, taking people off trains, preventing conversations. The practice not only returned, but is enriched with new means of pressure on the people."

Soldatov and Borogan recount how under Russian President Boris Yeltsin, journalists experienced greater freedom to investigate the crimes committed by the Soviet regime. But they note that this freedom was short-lived, explaining how under Putin the internal security apparatus reverted to the use of "police state" methods to suppress the exercise of journalistic freedoms.

The authors provide a chilling description of the FSB's approach to countering the threat of terrorism, citing incidents that reflect what they portray as official incompetence. For example, they detail the events that transpired during the 2002 Moscow theater siege in which Chechen terrorists took more than 1,000 hostages. Russian special forces working with the FSB raided the theater using fentanyl gas to subdue the hostage-takers. Use of the gas resulted in the death of 130 hostages. The authors, eye-witnesses to the unfolding drama, describe the FSB's "frightening lack of preparedness" to deal with the situation and explain how – despite official assertions that the theater siege represented a "victory" against terrorism – the FSB "had mounted an ill-coordinated operation and managed to bungle it."

In an example of the FSB's failure to learn from its previous mistakes, a 2004 terrorist attack on a school in Beslan resulted in the taking of more than 1,100 hostages, including 770 children. The authors explain how the FSB was unprepared for the events that transpired, which ultimately led to the storming of the building and the deaths of 334 hostages, including 186 children.

Beyond the FSB's role in suppressing internal dissent, Soldatov and Borogan document the security services' role in "extrajudicial killings," assassinations abroad (the poisoning in London of Alexander Litvinenko with radioactive Polonium-210 was a celebrated case), and in implementing the policy of "counter-capture," i.e., the seizure of a suspected terrorist's relatives to encourage his surrender and to deter future terrorist attacks.

For those who had high hopes that post-Soviet Russia would move steadily toward joining the ranks of fully democratic nations, "The New Nobility" is both illuminating and disheartening. As the authors note, the inability to establish and solidify the rule of law is "one of the most profound failures of Russia in the years after the end of Communism." Unfortunately, the state security services have been "caught up in the practices of earlier times, escaping accountability and serving as an agent of the state rather than of the law."

Old habits may indeed be the most difficult to break, and Russia's "new nobility" may be the most reluctant to break them. But at least there are courageous Russian journalists like Soldatov and Borogan willing to expose those habits to the rest of the world. Hopefully, their voices will continue to be heard.

Palestine's Self-Inflicted Catastrophe

SAMARA GREENBERG

A review of
Palestine Betrayed
by Efraim Karsh
2010 Yale University Press

W hen it comes to the birth of the Palestinian-Israeli conflict, the Palestinian narrative has become the most widely repeated version of events: After World War I, Jews began immigrating to areas within Britain's Mandate of Palestine with the Zionist dream of building a Jewish state. Jewish immigration dramatically increased at the end of World War II as a result of collective European guilt in the aftermath of the Holocaust. The Jews eventually established Israel as their illegal state after evicting the Arab population and plundering the Palestinian people and their homeland with the help of colonialist Europe. Israel's independence is known in Arabic as the *Nakba*—the

Samara Greenberg is a research associate and assistant editor for *inFocus Quarterly* at the Jewish Policy Center based in Washington, DC.

great catastrophe—and it created the Palestinian refugee problem, the biggest obstacle to solving the conflict today.

Enter Efraim Karsh, head of Mediterranean Studies at King's College London, and his latest book, *Palestine Betrayed.* A preeminent historian on the Arab-Israeli conflict, Karsh sets out "to reclaim the historical truth" behind Israel's creation. In doing so, he tests such Palestinian narratives and the conclusions of the "new historians"— revisionists such as Avi Shlaim, Ilan Pappe, and the early Benny Morris who in the 1980s rose to challenge the established narrative of Israel's birth.

Karsh sets the record straight by drawing on Western, United Nations, Israeli, and Soviet documents declassified over the last decade, providing the correct context often missing in the selective focus of the "new historians," and altogether absent in the Palestinian narrative. His detailed examination of the historical records reveals that Israel's establishment was not the main cause of the Palestinian refugee problem and the hardships that the population has faced thereafter. Instead, it was the result of actions taken by the Palestinian Arabs and their leaders.

Anger instigated by Arab leaders is the foremost reccurring theme in *Palestine Betrayed,* and Karsh holds the mufti of Jerusalem, Hajj Amin Husseini, responsible for the deterioration of neighborly relations between the Arabs and Jews during the Mandate period, and for the eventual "collapse and dispersion of Palestinian Arab society."

Hajj Amin, known for his pan-Arab ambitions, "viewed the Palestinians *not* as a distinct people deserving statehood but as an integral part of a single Arab nation"—with himself as leader, and clean of Jews. To this end, Hajj Amin, an admirer and supporter of Adolf Hitler's Nazi Germany, launched a campaign to demolish the Jewish national revival by enraging his constituents with all the anti-Jewish rhetoric he could find, from verses in the Quran to *The Protocols of the Elders of Zion.*

But the Mufti was not alone in his aspirations to control Palestine at the expense of its inhabitants. It was Transjordanian King Abdullah's "imperial ambitions" that eventually forced the newly formed Arab states to invade the day-old Israel in 1948, "not to save the Palestinian

By the end of the Mandate in May 1948, some 340,000 Arabs had fled Palestine; by January 1949, that number swelled to 600,000—a direct result of Arab leaders' coercion and invasion.

Arabs but to prevent the annexation of Palestine, in whole or in part, to Transjordan." Karsh astutely points out that the Arab invasion following Israel's independence "was more of a scramble for Palestine than an attempt to secure Palestinian national rights."

However, instead of consolidating Arab rule over Palestine, "The 1948 war resulted in the total disintegration of Palestinian Arab society." By the end of the Mandate in May 1948, some 340,000 Arabs had fled Palestine; by January 1949, that number swelled to 600,000—a direct result of Arab leaders' coercion and invasion.

Indeed, the Mufti and heads of surrounding Arab countries were largely responsible for the flight of the Palestinian Arabs—a highly controversial point that Karsh proves remarkably well with a substantial body of sourced material and quotations from key British, Jewish, and Arab eyewitnesses. While there were instances in which Jewish forces expelled Arab villagers in the heat of battle, in most cases, Arab leaders and their armed militias forcefully drove the Palestinian Arabs from their homes, at first to use the houses as military bases and then to prevent them from becoming citizens of a prospective Jewish state. Many others fled of their own free will as the wartime security situation deteriorated.

At the heart of *Palestine Betrayed*, Karsh argues that the Palestinian people were—and still are—betrayed by their very own leaders who promised to act with their best interests in mind but instead acted on personal ambitions. Never relinquishing their dreams of a pan-Arab empire under their homage, each leader refused to establish peaceful relations with the Jews, condemning the Palestinian people to decades of war and statelessness.

"Had the Mufti chosen to lead his people to peace and reconciliation with their Jewish neighbors," Karsh writes, "the Palestinians would have had their independent state" in accordance with the 1947 UN Partition Plan for Palestine, which the Jews accepted and Palestine's Arab leaders did not.

The same applied to Yassir Arafat in the late 1990s and early 2000s, when he chose to pocket international aid and create terrorist networks rather than infrastructure necessary for an independent state. The same now applies to Mahmoud Abbas who refuses to accept Israel's 'Jewishness' in a peace agreement but insists that Israel fully implement the right of return, "the Palestinian and Arab euphemism for Israel's destruction."

Palestine Betrayed is an extraordinarily well-documented account of the events leading up to Israel's creation. It is the antidote to revisionist historians whose narrative casts the Palestinians as passive players in the conflict with no responsibility for their actions. The contexts of war and inter-Arab rivalry are the key components to understanding how events played out. At the same time, Karsh's work demonstrates that Palestinian mythology continues to hinder all attempts at solving the Palestinian-Israeli conflict. Indeed, the notion that Israel is solely responsible for creating the Palestinian refugee encourages Palestinian leaders and society to cling to the erroneous belief that Israel will welcome each refugee into the state as part of a peace deal. And as long as this remains a Palestinian redline, there is no hope for ending the conflict.

The Arab World's Men in Washington

KYLE SHIDELER

A review of
The Arab Lobby: the Invisible Alliance that Undermines America's Interests in the Middle East

by Mitchell Bard

2010 HarperCollins

O ne of the key questions raised by Mitchell Bard's *The Arab Lobby: the Invisible Alliance that Undermines America's Interests in the Middle East* is: why are there so few Arabs in the Arab Lobby?

How is it that in Washington D.C., a curious mixture of state department officials, Texas oil men, academics, and missionaries should come together in order to argue the case on behalf of a handful of Arab states?

Bard's analysis begins with the early fights over Truman's decision to recognize the State of Israel, through the AWACs Arm Sales fight of the 1980s, and all the way to the present day. He documents how a disparate group of State Department apparatchiks, academics, missionary groups, professional K Street lobbyists and oil men, backed by

Kyle Shideler is the Senior Research Fellow at the Endowment for Middle East Truth (EMET).

petrodollars from the Arab States, have steadily worked to push America towards alliance with those states. Their ultimate goal? To have the United States accept the Arab view that Israel, as a pariah in the Middle East, is ultimately responsible for all the ills that bubble up from that region – whether the risk of Soviet influence, or the rise of radical Islam. Whatever the policy question, the only policy answer, it seems, is to stop supporting Israel.

The specter of *The Israel Lobby*, by Stephen Walt and John Mearsheimer, looms heavily over *The Arab Lobby* – it is readily apparent that Bard envisions the latter as a refutation of the claims advanced by the former. Bard accomplishes this objective in devastating detail. The premise of *The Israel Lobby* was that pro-Israel advocates dominated the Washington foreign policy discussion, and pushed hard to ensure an American alliance with the Jewish state – something that did the U.S. no favors in the international arena. No competitor existed, Walt and Mearsheimer asserted, that could compete against this pervasive Israeli lobby.

Following the publication of *The Arab Lobby*, however, such claims ought to be dismissed as bunk. The Arab lobby is alive and well, and gives as good as it gets.

For serious researchers of the Arab-Israeli policy battles, most of Bard's people, acronyms and stories of influence-peddling will already be deeply familiar. Ambassadors James Akins and Walter Cutler, lobbyists J. Crawford Cook and Tom Loeffler, and former CIA officer Raymond Close all turn up. So too does the alphabet soup of think tanks and non-profits, including the AAI (Arab American Institute), the ADC (American-Arab Anti-Discrimination Committee), the AMEU (Americans for Middle East Understanding), CNI (Council for the National Interest) and MEI (Middle East Institute). Lobbying and P.R. firms such as Qorvis Communications and Burston-Marsteller, among many others, also appear.

For the layman, the growing laundry list of people and organizations who have at one time or another served the Arab Lobby can prove difficult to follow. Fortunately, Bard has divided the book up practically, into a series of chapters that examine the growth of

The Arab Lobby represents not a genuine constituency of large numbers of Americans, but rather the political muscle of self appointed "Middle East experts," in the diplomatic, business and academic fields.

the lobby both chronologically and topically, including the rise of the Arabist wing of the State Department, the growth of Middle Eastern Studies departments as political indoctrination centers for the Lobby, and the history of activist Christian anti-Zionism.

Unlike other books which have broached this subject in recent years, most notably Craig Unger's *House of Bush, House of Saud* – which became the basis for Michael Moore's film *Fahrenheit 9/11* – there is little partisanship from Bard. He takes pains to make clear that the Arab Lobby has never distinguished between administrations, Republican or Democratic. Rather it has made efforts to insure equal access regardless of the party in power. Rewards for cooperation have extended to the generous funding of libraries and foundations of former Presidents Jimmy Carter, George H.W. Bush and Bill Clinton.

While establishing that the Arab Lobby exists, Bard also seeks to establish that the lobby's activities and intentions are, to use his term, "nefarious." He argues convincingly that the Arab Lobby represents not a genuine constituency of large numbers of Americans, but rather the political muscle of self appointed "Middle East experts," in the diplomatic, business and academic fields. He shows this through convincing public opinion polls, in which the American public in general has largely favored Israel by wider margins than their Arab neighbors. The Arab Lobby represents a disturbingly undemocratic influence on foreign policy making.

Unfortunately this distinction – the one between Pro-Israel sentiments being grassroots based, versus an Arab Lobby which seeks to impose its elitist view in contrast to the people's preferences – means Bard gives something of a pass to several of the prominent Muslim organizations.

Bard does cover the revelations of the Holy Land Foundation terrorism funding trial, which definitively proved the massive extent of activity by the Muslim Brotherhood, including its influence operations to gain access to American officials, and its fundraising for Hamas. But Bard minimizes the extent of this evident damage.

For instance, while Bard does an excellent job in recounting the evidence against the Council on American Islamic Relations as a Muslim Brotherhood group – including pointing to its support for terrorism against Israel, its foreign fundraising, and its efforts to browbeat and intimidate Americans concerned about the risk of radical Islam – he fails to document other organizations and individuals which were also named as Muslim Brotherhood outfits, in the same Holy Land Foundation trial.

Those organizations include the Islamic Society of North America (ISNA), the Islamic Circle of North America (ICNA), the International Institute for Islamic Thought (IIIT), the Muslim American Society (MAS) and the North American Islamic Trust (NAIT), which are all named in Bard's book, but not defined as members of the Brotherhood. It is disappointing that instead of pulling the veil back on these groups, Bard attempts to minimize the reality of this threat.

He says, "The vast majority of American Muslims are exercising their democratic right to participate in the political process," and "Legitimate Muslim organizations are outraged by the behavior of radical groups such as the Holy Land foundation…" Yet he cites only the opinion of Dr. Zuhdi Jasser, founder of the American Islamic Forum for Democracy (AIFD) as representative of this silent majority. And while the work done by Dr. Jasser and the AIFD is absolutely commendable, it is the Muslim Brotherhood-backed groups which hold Iftar dinners at the White House.

Hesitance to engage on the issue of the Muslim Brotherhood aside, Bard's *Arab Lobby* represents an essential piece of work. Bard names and shames those who have, from 1948 to the present, engaged in a steady stream of influence – counter to the expressed wishes of the American public – aimed at driving a wedge between America and its democratic ally Israel, for the betterment of Israel's despotic Arab neighbors. *The Arab Lobby* successfully documents the clashes between lobbies, and gives a disturbing glimpse into the manner in which Middle East foreign policy is often made.

Shariah 101

CHRISTOPHER HOLTON

A review of
Shariah Law for Non-Muslims
by the Center for the Study of Political Islam
2010 CSPI, LLC

J ust three years ago, the Family Security Group commissioned a polling organization to conduct a survey. One of the questions asked in that survey was, "Have you heard of Shariah law?"

Only 3% of respondents claimed to have even heard the term "Shariah".

Today, many more Americans have heard of Shariah. Shariah is not quite a household name at this point, but it is a term that is now used widely in news stories and on talk radio.

But do Americans *really* know what Shariah is? Where can they go to find out more about this foreign (in every sense of the word) doctrine which has insinuated itself in Western society's culture and legal systems?

Christopher Holton is a Vice President with the Center for Security Policy. Mr. Holton previously served as president and marketing director of Blanchard & Co., and was editor-in-chief of the Blanchard Economic Research Unit from 1990-2003.

Although there are several good books on the subject, most Americans simply do not have the time nor the inclination to sit down and read a 300-page book on Shariah law. Still, Americans have a need to know what Shariah is, given that Shariah is both the enemy threat doctrine in the global Jihadist insurgency we are fighting against today, as well as the central goal of Islamic Jihadist groups as diverse as the Muslim Brotherhood, Al Qaeda, Hezbollah, HAMAS, the Taliban, Lashkar-e-Taiba, Hizb-ut-Tahrir, Abu Sayyef, Jemmaah Islamiyah, Tabligi Jamaat and Jamaat ul Fuqra.

Fortunately, Dr. Bill Warner has provided an excellent means through which Americans can learn about Shariah: the 44-page primer, *Sharia Law for Non-Muslims.*

Sharia Law for Non-Muslims is ideal for educating most people about Shariah. Written in a concise, intelligent, yet non-intimidating format, this primer is entirely accessible, even for readers with no background in Islam, Shariah or law.

Dr. Warner is also perhaps the ideal author for such a publication. He has traveled extensively across America delivering hundreds of lectures on what he terms "political Islam." One of his most impressive accomplishments is a publication called "A Simple Koran." This book is an English translation of the Koran in which Dr. Warner also performed the tedious and unprecedented task of ordering the Koran chronologically. Dr. Warner has written 13 other books on Islam and also produced a self-study course on Political Islam available on CD.

Sharia Law for Non-Muslims is broken down into eleven chapters covering the vital aspects of Shariah, including:

- What is Shariah?
- Women under Shariah
- Family law in Shariah
- Kafirs (non-believers) under Shariah
- Jihad
- Shariah and slavery
- Shariah-Compliant Finance

Among the most useful sections of Sharia Law for Non-Muslims are those that touch on some of Warner's most significant overall work: a statistical analysis of Islamic doctrine and literature.

Warner draws on his previous analyses of all of the major sources of Islamic doctrine today to provide important details, such as:

- The percentage of text in Islamic doctrine devoted to Non-believers (Kafirs)
- The percentage of text in Islamic doctrine devoted to Jihad
- A statistical breakdown of the status of women as portrayed in Islamic texts

These statistical analyses provide direct insight into the nature of Shariah and its relevance to non-Muslims and the West in general.

Readers will not only find *Sharia Law for Non-Muslims* to be a valuable introduction to Shariah law, but will also find it to be a good starting point for exploring the broader and more detailed work from the Center for the Study of Political Islam.

For more information on the Center for the Study of Political Islam, visit politicalislam.com.